Everyday Japanese

Delicious Homemade Recipes

BY: Valeria Ray

License Notes

A Special Reward for Purchasing My Book!

Thank you, cherished reader, for purchasing my book and taking the time to read it. As a special reward for your decision, I would like to offer a gift of free and discounted books directly to your inbox. All you need to do is fill in the box below with your email address and name to start getting amazing offers in the comfort of your own home. You will never miss an offer because a reminder will be sent to you. Never miss a deal and get great deals without having to leave the house! Subscribe now and start saving!

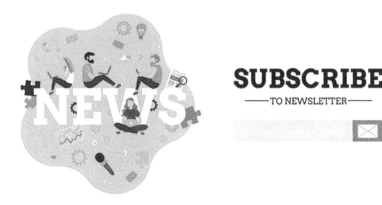

https://valeria-ray.gr8.com

Contents

Simple and Delicious Japanese Food Recipes

MMMMMMMMMMMMMMMMMMMMMMMMMMMMMMMMMMM

Chapter I - Japanese Noodle Recipes

MMMMMMMMMMMMMMMMMMMMMMMMMMMMMMMMMM

(1) Spicy Shirataki Salad

Noodle salads are a big thing in Japan. They make for a nice side dish or appetizer. With its low-calorie content, shirataki is often used as a diet meal and this tasty recipe would fit right into the category. It will fill you up minus the worries of gaining weight.

Yield: 2

Cooking Time: 20 mins

List of Ingredients:

- 1 packet shirataki, cooked according to package directions
- ½ cup cooked ham, cut into strips
- 6 pcs cherry tomatoes, halved
- 1/3 cucumber, peeled, seeded, and cut into strips
- 1 pc carrot, peeled and cut into strips
- 2 tablespoons rice vinegar
- ¾ tablespoons mirin
- ½ tablespoons sesame oil
- 4 tablespoons soy sauce
- 1/3 teaspoons mustard powder
- ½ teaspoons chilli paste
- Ground pepper to taste

MMMMMMMMMMMMMMMMMMMMMMMMMMMMMMMMMM

Methods:

1. Mix all the sauce ingredients together in a bowl until well combined. Set aside.

2. Cut up cooked shirataki noodles into smaller lengths so they are easier to eat.

3. Mix noodles together with the vegetables.

4. Toss in soy dressing and coat the salad with it.

5. Serve.

(2) Classic Tokyo Ramen

The ramen recipe has been adapted all over the world, producing a bunch of variants, which also include instant, no-cook types. But if you want the authentic taste, you have to go back to how they make it in Tokyo. It's a serious project that involves intricate procedures. You have to be ready for a workout just so you can make the rich and hearty bowl. But this is a modern world and we live in fast-paced generation. That's why we made it simpler and quicker to make.

Yield: 4

Cooking Time: 35 mins

List of Ingredients:

- 13 oz. ramen noodles, cooked according to package directions
- 2 cups fried pork, sliced into strips
- 3 cloves garlic, divided
- 2 tablespoons ginger, sliced
- 1 cup baby spinach leaves
- 3 cups chicken stock
- 1 teaspoon Worcestershire sauce
- 4 tablespoons soy sauce
- ½ teaspoons five spice powder
- 1 teaspoon white sugar
- Pinch of chilli powder
- 2 pcs hard-boiled eggs, peeled and halved
- 1 sheet nori seaweed paper, sliced
- 4 tablespoons corn kernels
- 1 tablespoon spring onions, shaved into thin strips
- 1 teaspoon sesame seeds, toasted

MMMMMMMMMMMMMMMMMMMMMMMMMMMMMMMMM

Methods:

1. Sauté crushed 1 clove of garlic in sesame oil. Add sliced pork and a tablespoon of soy sauce. Cook for a couple of minutes until the flavors blend together. Transfer in bowl and set aside.

2. Place the remaining garlic cloves, cut in half, in a stockpot.

3. Add chicken stock, Worcestershire sauce, remaining 3 tablespoons of soy sauce, and ginger. Season with five spice and chili powder. Boil over medium heat, then, reduce to low and simmer for about 5 minutes.

4. Adjust the seasoning according to your preference.

5. To assemble, divide noodles into four bowls. Top with seasoned fried pork, spinach leaves, and corn kernels.

6. Scoop simmering hot soup stock.

7. Sprinkle with nori sheets and sesame seeds before serving.

(3) Hiyamugi and Japanese Pickles

Hiyamugi are prepared and served the same as somen, usually as a cold side dish spiced with a soy and dashi dressing. For this recipe, hiyamugi noodles are served together with pickled Japanese favorites, which help enhance the bland taste. You can either make the pickles or buy them in bottled form at an Asian grocer. Finding them is not that difficult.

Yield: 4

Cooking Time: 30 mins

List of Ingredients:

- 10 oz. hiyamugi, cooked according to package directions
- ½ cup pickled daikon
- ½ cup pickled ginger
- ½ cup pickled Asian mushrooms
- ½ cup soy sauce
- ½ cup mirin
- 5cm-piece kombu kelp
- ½ teaspoons bonito flakes
- 2 cups water
- 1 tablespoon spring onions, chopped
- 1 tablespoon shisho leaves, chopped

MMMMMMMMMMMMMMMMMMMMMMMMMMMMMMMM

Methods:

1. Boil water, kombu kelp, and bonito flakes in a saucepan over medium heat.

2. Strain mixture in a fine sieve and discard the solids.

3. Boil mixture again for a few minutes. Transfer to a bowl and allow to chill for about 20 minutes.

4. Place hiyamugi in a bowl. Garnish with shisho leaves and spring onions.

5. Serve chilled noodles with prepared dipping sauce and pickled daikon, pickled ginger, and pickled Asian mushrooms in separate bowls.

(4) Stir-Fried Seafood Udon

Yakiudon is a popular Japanese noodle dish that is widely enjoyed in instant form. But of course, tasting the real thing is an entirely different experience you would surely love. Udon, with its thick chewy texture, easily comes to life once a couple of other ingredients are thrown into the wok, along with spices and sauces that will further make it interesting. There are no limits as to the choice of ingredients you would want to put into your udon. That's the beauty of cooking it. You can use whatever is available, even picking from a leftover recipe. For this version, seafood is the focus although there are some bits of meat for additional umami. Let's go!

Yield: 2

Cooking Time: 15 mins

List of Ingredients:

- 14 oz. udon, cooked according to package directions
- 4 oz. pork tenderloin, cut into thin strips
- 4 pcs prawns, peeled and deveined
- 4-8 pcs scallops, shelled and rinsed
- ¼ cup carrots, cut into strips
- ¼ cup cabbage, chopped
- 1 pc white onion, chopped
- 3 cloves garlic, crushed
- ¼ cup shiitake mushrooms
- 2 pcs hard-boiled egg, peeled and halved
- 1 tablespoon Japanese mayonnaise
- 1 teaspoon dashi stock
- 2 teaspoons sweet cooking sake
- 3 teaspoons soy sauce
- 1 tablespoon vegetable oil
- Salt and pepper to taste

MMMMMMMMMMMMMMMMMMMMMMMMMMMMMMMMM

Methods:

1. Heat oil in a wok over medium fire.

2. Sauté garlic for about a minute. Add onions and stir continuously until the onions are translucent, about 2 minutes.

3. Add pork and stir-fry for 5-10 minutes until slightly brown.

4. Stir in shrimps. Continue cooking, stirring frequently, until the shrimps change in color.

5. Add scallops and cook for another two minutes.

6. Cook veggies next before adding the rest of the ingredients. Mixing until well combined.

7. Serve.

(5) Harusame Spring Rolls

Spring rolls are a hit in Asia and these Japanese style spring rolls would surely make your tummy happy. It's a delightful mix of vegetables and harusame noodles. With no meat in the recipe, it's a great dish for vegans.

Yield: 4

Cooking Time: 30 mins

List of Ingredients:

- 1 packet harusame, cooked according to package directions
- 8 sheets spring roll wrappers
- 1 pc carrot, cut into strips
- 2 pcs green bell peppers, cut into strips
- 5 pcs shiitake mushrooms, sliced
- 1 tablespoon soy sauce
- 1 tablespoon sesame oil
- Salt to taste
- Vegetable oil for frying

MMMMMMMMMMMMMMMMMMMMMMMMMMMMMMMMMM

Methods:

1. Heat sesame oil in a wok over medium fire.

2. Stir-fry vegetables until soft.

3. Add cooked harusame and continue to mix until combined.

4. Season with salt and soy sauce. Continue stirring until vegetables are cooked. Transfer into a bowl and allow to cool.

5. Spoon harusame and veggie filling in a spring roll wrapper, spreading evenly on one side.

6. Carefully roll the wrapper. Seal the edges with a bit of water and flour mixture.

7. Fry spring rolls in hot oil until brown on both sides.

8. Serve.

(6) Salmon and Soba in Miso Soup

Fresh salmon fillets are delectable as is. If you add them into a soba noodle miso soup, the result is nothing but delicious. This recipe is very easy to make, requires only 8 ingredients, and come out very tasty. It's a great dish for those cold winter nights and then some.

Yield: 4

Cooking Time: 25 mins

List of Ingredients:

- 9 oz. soba, cooked according to package directions
- 4 pcs salmon fillets
- 4 servings instant miso soup
- 4 cups baby spinach
- 1 teaspoon wasabi paste
- 1/3 cup Japanese mayonnaise
- 1 tablespoon vegetable oil
- 6 cups water
- ½ teaspoons sesame seeds, toasted
- Sea salt flakes to taste

MMMMMMMMMMMMMMMMMMMMMMMMMMMMMM

Methods:

1. Rub sea salt flakes on salmon fillets, then, panfry in vegetable oil skin side down, for about 3 minutes per side.

2. Boil water in a stockpot over medium fire.

3. Add miso soup, stirring frequently until smooth.

4. Stir in soba and spinach. Cook for another minute until spinach has wilted.

5. Serve with combined wasabi paste and mayonnaise in a small bowl. Serve hot.

(7) Vinegared Torokoten Noodles

With its jelly texture and light flavor, torokoten has become a favorite dessert ingredient. It blends well with a bit of sugar and naturally sweet fruits to make a delicious, refreshing, and healthy snack. But the traditional way of serving this Japanese specialty noodles is with a spiced vinegar sauce. Follow the recipe below.

Yield: 2

Cooking Time: 10 mins

List of Ingredients:

- 1 cup torokoten noodles, cooked according to package directions
- ¼ cup vinegar
- 2 teaspoons soy sauce
- 1 teaspoon sesame oil
- 1 tablespoon ginger, grated
- 1 pc nori sheet, cut into small pieces
- 1 tablespoon shisho leaves, chopped

MMMMMMMMMMMMMMMMMMMMMMMMMMMMMMMMMMM

Methods:

1. Combine together all the sauce ingredients in a bowl.

2. Add torokoten and mix until combined.

3. Garnish with grated ginger, shisho leaves, and nori.

4. Serve.

(8) Tasty Somen Cooler

Summer in Japan is pretty humid. When you want a dish that will cool you down, this somen recipe is the right pick. It is refreshing and delectable and could instantly ease your hotness.

Yield: 4

Cooking Time: 15 mins

List of Ingredients:

- 1 lb. dried somen, cooked according to package instructions
- 2 cups dashi stock
- ¼ cup light soy sauce
- 2 tablespoons mirin
- 1 ½ cup Japanese soy sauce
- 2 tablespoons fresh ginger, grated
- 1 pc scallion, chopped
- ½ cup shiso leaves, sliced

MMMMMMMMMMMMMMMMMMMMMMMMMMMMMMMMM

Methods:

1. Combine seasoning together in a small bowl, mixing until well combined.

2. Garnish dipping sauce with grated ginger, sliced shiso leaves, and chopped scallions.

3. Serve cooked somen noodles chilled together with the dipping sauce.

Chapter II - Japanese Rice Recipes

MMMMMMMMMMMMMMMMMMMMMMMMMMMMMMMMMM

(9) Temaki Rolls

We heard you, the complication in preparing sushi rolls can be daunting. To help relieve your stress, here's a temaki recipe. Instead of sushi rolls cut from a delicate log of rolled rice with filling, this one is made in a cone-shaped nori sheet package. This is much easier to make but equally satisfying, we assure you. It's a great recipe to prepare for the appetizer spread at the buffet table.

Yield: 6

Cooking Time: 20 mins

List of Ingredients:

- 4 cups cooked sushi rice
- 4 pcs nori sheets, cut into 6 equal rectangles
- ½ cup ripe mango, thinly sliced
- ½ cup ripe avocado, thinly sliced
- ¼ cup caviar
- 4 oz. smoked salmon, sliced into strips
- 4 oz. prawns, cooked and sliced

MMMMMMMMMMMMMMMMMMMMMMMMMMMMMMMMMM

Methods:

1. Lay a rectangle-shaped nori sheet, shiny side down in your prep counter.

2. Add a tablespoon of rice and spread evenly, occupying a 45-degree angle at the center.

3. Top with your choice of fillings.

4. Roll temaki carefully to make a sushi cone.

5. Repeat with the rest of the ingredients.

6. Serve.

(10) Sushi Rolls

There are a variety of sushi roll recipes available. The most basic is the one with fresh tuna and salmon filling. But you can go as creative as you can with the ingredients as well as the look of your sushi. You can even make one that is done inside and out, meaning the rice is placed in the middle, just like the salmon in the original version. To give you a head start on sushi making, we will provide the most basic recipe here.

Yield: 6

Cooking Time: 55 mins

List of Ingredients:

- 5 pcs nori sheets
- 2 oz. salmon, sushi-grade class, cut into strips
- 2 oz. tuna, sushi-grade class, cut into strips
- ½ avocado, cut into thin strips
- 1 pc cucumber, julienned
- 1 pc carrot, julienned

For Sushi Rice:

- 5 cups short-grain Japanese rice, rinsed and drained
- ½ cup rice vinegar
- 6 cups water
- 2 tablespoons sugar
- 1 teaspoon salt

MMMMMMMMMMMMMMMMMMMMMMMMMMMMMMMM

Methods:

1. Cook sushi rice by boiling rice with 6 cups of water in a saucepan with a tight lid over medium fire.

2. Allow water to boil for 3 minutes before reducing heat to low, simmering rice without taking the lid, until liquid is absorbed completely, about 15 minutes.

3. Once cooked, transfer rice in a cookie sheet.

4. Stir in vinegar, salt, and sugar, then, mix until well combined. Allow to cool, covered with damp paper towels, before starting to make sushi.

5. Arrange a piece of nori sheet, shiny side down in a bamboo rolling mat. Make about 1 inch of allowance on the portion closest to you.

6. Get a handful of rice and spread it in the center of the nori sheet. Top it with veggies and fish, then, roll the sushi carefully, making sure it is held firmly.

7. Repeat the process with the remaining ingredients.

8. Slice each log into 5-6 pieces and serve.

(11) Sushi Cups

This is another creative way to serve everybody's favorite sushi. It's a spectacle from the presentation to the taste and would be an ideal addition to a buffet spread. Just like with other sushi recipes, you can prepare a wide range of filling choices, depending on your preference or that of your guests.

Yield: 6

Cooking Time: 20 mins

List of Ingredients:

- 4 cups cooked sushi rice
- ½ cup ripe mango, thinly sliced
- ½ cup ripe avocado, thinly sliced
- ¼ cup caviar
- 4 oz. smoked salmon, flaked
- 4 oz. prawns, cooked and diced
- 1 cup egg omelet, thinly sliced

MMMMMMMMMMMMMMMMMMMMMMMMMMMMMMMMMMMM

Methods:

1. Use shot glasses to make 4-5 alternating layers of sushi rice and your choice of fillings.

2. Top with egg omelet.

(12) Japanese Rice Balls

Another rice delicacy that the Japanese love and is a scene-stealer in their meals is these rice balls. They are made into either triangle or round shapes and are often added into bento lunchboxes. As a standalone snack, rice balls may also be eaten alone like a bun. In fact, there are food trucks selling these delightful rice balls, which are grilled and seasoned with nori, sesame seeds, salt, and sugar. They may also be made with a filling composed of either meat, fish, or pickled plums and other veggies.

Yield: 8

Cooking Time: 35 mins

List of Ingredients:

- 4 cups cooked Japanese rice
- 1 pc dried nori sheets, cut into strips
- ½ teaspoons black sesame seeds, toasted
- Pinch of salt

For the Filling:

- Pickled plum
- Salted salmon, grilled and cut into chunks

MMMMMMMMMMMMMMMMMMMMMMMMMMMMMMMM

Methods:

1. Put ½ cup of rice in a bowl.

2. Season with sesame seeds and salt, then, mix by hand until rice is well seasoned.

3. Place your chosen filling onto rice, push lightly between your palms and form into your desired shape.

4. Wrap the rice ball with a strip of nori sheet, sprinkle with toasted sesame seeds.

5. Serve.

(13) Karaage Bento

Bento lunchboxes have been making waves in the food industry. Homemakers and professional cooks alike mastered the artful way of preparing lunch to make them more inviting and easily satisfying. Japanese bentos are a treat to the eyes as much as they are to the tummies. They will definitely please even the most discriminating tastes and the hardest-to-please diners.

Yield: 4

Cooking Time: 1 hr 35 mins

List of Ingredients:

For the Side Dishes:

- 4 pcs Japanese rice balls
- 1 cup broccoli florets, steamed
- 1 cup corn kernels and spinach sautéed in butter
- 4 pcs rolled omelet

For Karaage:

- 1 lb. chicken thighs, cut into serving pieces
- 1 teaspoon ginger, crushed
- 8 garlic cloves, minced
- 1 teaspoon granulated sugar
- ¼ cup all purpose flour
- ¼ cup potato starch
- 1 tablespoon soy sauce
- 1 teaspoon sesame oil
- 1 tablespoon dry sherry
- Salt and pepper to taste
- Vegetable oil for frying

MMMMMMMMMMMMMMMMMMMMMMMMMMMMMMMMMMM

Methods:

1. Marinade chicken thighs in ginger, garlic, soy sauce, sesame oil, and dry sherry. Season with salt and pepper.

2. Place chicken with the marinade in a Ziploc bag and chill for at least an hour until the meat absorbs the flavors.

3. Mix flour and potato starch in a bowl.

4. Drench chicken in flour mixture, then, fry in hot oil over medium fire until golden brown.

5. Drain in paper towels.

6. For the rice, kindly refer to the Japanese rice balls recipe above.

7. To assemble your bento box, cut up your karaage and side dishes according to your preference. Neatly arrange them in a lunch box and serve.

(14) Japanese Fried Rice

Just like with other cuisines, the Japanese have their own, unique way of preparing fried rice. This one hits close to home. It features the basic Japanese flavor provided by soy sauce and a handful of colorful veggies plus scrambled eggs for a nice finish. Don't worry. The recipe is quite simple, very easy to follow, and provides a delicious result.

Yield: 4

Cooking Time: 40 mins

List of Ingredients:

- 4 cups Japanese rice, cooked
- ½ cup onion, diced
- 2 tablespoons carrots, diced
- 1 cup frozen peas, thawed
- 2 eggs, cooked scrambled style and diced into bits
- 1 ½ tablespoons butter
- 2 tablespoons soy sauce
- Salt and pepper to taste

MMMMMMMMMMMMMMMMMMMMMMMMMMMMMMMMMMM

Methods:

1. Combine cooked rice with thawed peas, and diced onions and carrots. Mix well.

2. Heat butter in a wok over medium fire.

3. Add rice with veggies. Tossing continuously until heated through.

4. Season with soy sauce, salt, and pepper to taste.

5. Add scrambled egg bits and mix until combined.

6. Serve warm.

(15) Salmon and Sticky Coconut Rice

Salmon is a favorite fish in Japan and it's quite obvious why! They have plenty of fresh supply that they use to make delightful lunches and dinners. This sticky coconut rice paired with sesame salmon is a well-balanced meal that could surely delight your family's tummies.

Yield: 4

Cooking Time: 40 mins

List of Ingredients:

- 4 pcs boneless salmon fillets
- 2 cups Akafuji Akitakomachi rice, rinsed
- ½ cup pickled cucumber, sliced into ribbons
- 1 pc red chilli, thinly sliced
- 1 tablespoon fresh ginger, grated
- 1 tablespoon clear honey
- ½ tablespoons soy sauce
- 2 tablespoons sesame oil
- 1 can coconut milk
- 2 cups water
- 1 cup edamame beans, blanched
- 1 cup pea shoots
- 1 tablespoon sesame seeds, toasted

MMMMMMMMMMMMMMMMMMMMMMMMMMMMMMMMMM

Methods:

1. Combine coconut milk and water in a medium, heavy-bottomed saucepan. Bring to a boil over medium heat.

2. Add rice and stir.

3. Bring to a boil, then, lower heat and cook rice in a simmer for about 10 minutes.

4. While rice is cooking, marinade salmon in a mixture of sesame oil, soy sauce, honey, ginger, and chili. Leave on for at least 15 minutes.

5. Preheat the grill and prepare an aluminum foil lined baking dish.

6. Place marinated salmon, skin side down and cook for a total of 10 minutes, turning once and basting with some of the marinade while grilling.

7. To serve, divide sticky coconut rice onto plates, top with salmon fillets, and place a side dish of pickled cucumbers, edamame beans, and pea shoots on the side. Sprinkle with toasted sesame seeds.

(16) Peas and Rice

Japanese rice is pretty versatile. You can always add a little something to serve it differently and bust the boredom of eating it. If you want a special way to serve rice at the dining table, try this Japanese style peas and rice recipe. It features only a handful of ingredients but could make a lot of difference, especially since the rice is flavored with sake or rice wine, dashi stock, and mirin.

Yield: 3

Cooking Time: 30 mins

List of Ingredients:

- 1 ½ cups Japanese rice, rinsed
- ¾ cup peas
- 3 cups water, divided
- 2 ½ tablespoons sake
- 1 teaspoon dashi stock
- 1 ½ teaspoons mirin
- 1 teaspoon salt, divided

MMMMMMMMMMMMMMMMMMMMMMMMMMMMMMMMM

Methods:

1. Boil peas in ½ cup of water seasoned with 1 tablespoon of sake and half a teaspoon of salt over medium fire. Cover and cook for 5-10 minutes.

2. Drain peas, reserving seasoned water, and set aside to cool.

3. Place reserved water from boiling peas in a rice cooker. Add the remaining 2 ½ cups of water, 1 ½ tablespoon of sake, dashi stock, and mirin.

4. Add rice and season with salt.

5. Cook for about 10-15 minutes or until rice is nice and fluffy.

6. Stir in cooked peas and serve.

Chapter III - Meat and Seafood:
Main Dish Favorites

MMMMMMMMMMMMMMMMMMMMMMMMMMMMMMMMMM

(17) Sake Beef Fillet

A good chunk of diced beef fillet, seasoned well with Japanese flavors. That's what this raw meat recipe is all about. Prepare it and you will discover why the locals love this so much.

Yield: 1

Cooking Time: 5 mins

List of Ingredients:

- 8 oz. beef, coarsely diced
- 5 pcs cornichons, diced
- 1 pc shallot, diced
- 1 pc egg yolk
- 3 tablespoons sake
- 2 teaspoons Dijon mustard
- 1 tablespoon parsley, finely diced
- 1 sprig flat leaf parsley, diced
- 4 pcs pea shoot tendrils

MMMMMMMMMMMMMMMMMMMMMMMMMMMMMMMMMM

Methods:

1. Combine all the ingredients in a bowl except for the parsley and pea shoots.

2. Form mixture into a rectangle.

3. Garnish with parsley and pea shoots. Serve.

(18) Prime Japanese Seafood Stew

If you want to showcase all the fresh seafood ingredients that Japan takes pride in, you may try making this seafood stew, usually made for special occasions. This one has scallops, squid, tuna, and prawns but you can always add up other ingredients you might like to make it heartier. It's a yummy recipe that's perfect for winter.

Yield: 4

Cooking Time: 40 mins

List of Ingredients:

- 8 pcs scallops
- 4 pcs tiger prawns, peeled and deveined
- 1 pc tuna fillet, cut into chunks
- 1 cup squid, cleaned and sliced
- 1 cup soba noodles, cooked according to package directions
- 1 cup bean sprouts
- 1 cup snow peas
- ¼ cup mushrooms
- 1 pc red bell pepper, sliced
- 1 tablespoon ginger, peeled and cut into strips
- 3 tablespoons soy sauce
- 2 tablespoons dry sherry
- Juice of 1 lime
- 5 cups chicken stock

MMMMMMMMMMMMMMMMMMMMMMMMMMMMMMMMMMMM

Methods:

1. Heat chicken stock in a pot. Stir in ginger and bring to a boil.

2. Add red bell peppers and mushrooms. Continue boiling, reduce heat to low, and simmer for 10 minutes.

3. Add tuna and cook for 5 minutes before adding the scallops.

4. After another 5 minutes, add the remaining ingredients except squid.

5. Simmer for 5 minutes, add squid slices, and boil for a minute.

6. Adjust seasoning according to taste.

7. Serve.

(19) Beef and Potatoes Stew

Meat and potatoes are favorite stew ingredients in Japan. This comfort food is inspired by that principle. It's light, simple to cook, and best eaten as the flavors meld together over time. It's a perfect make ahead recipe that you can reheat as many times and taste as delightful or even better afterwards.

Yield: 4

Cooking Time: 35 mins

List of Ingredients:

- ¾ lb. ground beef
- 1 ½ lbs. potatoes, peeled and cut into chunks
- 1 pc yellow onion, sliced
- 1 ½ tablespoons fresh ginger, peeled and minced
- 1 pc carrot, cut into chunks
- 1 cup chicken broth
- ½ cup water
- ¼ cup dry white wine
- ¼ cup soy sauce
- 2 tablespoons light brown sugar
- Salt to taste
- 2 pcs scallions, sliced diagonally

MMMMMMMMMMMMMMMMMMMMMMMMMMMMMMMM

Methods:

1. Brown beef in hot oil over medium fire, stirring frequently for two minutes.

2. Stir in onions, ginger, and carrots.

3. Whisk in dry white wine and simmer quickly to evaporate, scraping the bottom for browned bits.

4. Add the potatoes and the rest of the ingredients, except for the scallions.

5. Allow the stew to boil, reduce heat to low, and continue to cook in a simmer, until the potatoes and carrots are tender.

6. Garnish with sliced scallions before serving.

(20) Grilled Mackerel

One of the best ways to enjoy fresh seafood is lightly salting it and then, straight to the grill. That's exactly the idea for this recipe. It's simple, easy to make, and will surely showcase how fresh seafood in Japan is. If mackerel fillet is not available in your grocer, you can always substitute it with salmon.

Yield: 2

Cooking Time: 15 mins

List of Ingredients:

- 2 pcs mackerel fillets, halved
- Sea salt flakes to taste
- 1 pc Daikon radish, grated
- 1 pc lemon, sliced
- 3 tablespoons light soy sauce

MMMMMMMMMMMMMMMMMMMMMMMMMMMMMMMMMMMM

Methods:

1. Rub sea salt flakes onto fish fillets.

2. Arrange fish in an aluminum pan, skin side down, and broil for about 7-10 minutes.

3. Carefully turn fillets and cook for another 4 minutes to brown the skin.

4. Serve with a side dish of grated Daikon and lemon slices, plus soy sauce.

(21) Japanese-Style Ginger Pork

Pork is the Japan's favorite meat. In fact, it is the most consumed meat in the country, made into a bunch of sumptuous recipes. This simple ginger pork is one of those. It is quick and easy to make and delicious enough to make your dinners wonderful. If you are not fond of pork, you may substitute it for chicken.

Yield: 4

Cooking Time: 1 hr 20 mins

List of Ingredients:

- 1 lb. pork loin, thinly sliced
- 1 tablespoon fresh ginger, peeled and grated
- 2 tablespoons mirin
- 2 tablespoons sake
- 2 tablespoons soy sauce
- 3 tablespoons vegetable oil

MMMMMMMMMMMMMMMMMMMMMMMMMMMMMMMMMMMMMM

Methods:

1. Combine all the ingredients in a bowl, except for oil.

2. Allow pork to marinade for at least an hour.

3. When pork is almost ready, heat oil in a skillet at high.

4. Brown pork and cook until crispy.

(22) Crispy Prawns Tempura

Tempura is another national Japanese dish. It must be in your menu whenever you plan a Japanese dinner because the table spread would be lacking without it. Tempura could be served as an appetizer or a main dish, together with other battered treats like zucchini, carrots, and squash blossoms.

Yield: 6

Cooking Time: 15 mins

List of Ingredients:

- 1 lb. medium-sized prawns, peeled and deveined
- 2 tablespoons corn flour
- 1 cup all-purpose flour
- 1 pc egg yolk
- 2 pcs egg whites, lightly beaten
- 1 cup water
- Pinch of salt
- 2 cups vegetable oil

MMMMMMMMMMMMMMMMMMMMMMMMMMMMMMMM

Methods:

1. Preheat oil in the deep fryer until the temperature reaches 375 degrees F.

2. Combine all dry ingredients in a bowl. Make a well in the center.

3. Place water and egg yolk in the well, mixing until flour mixture is moistened, then, add egg whites.

4. Dip prepared prawns in the batter one at a time, carefully place in hot oil, and fry until crisp and golden.

5. Drain tempura on paper towel lined plates.

6. Serve on its own, or with a side of your choice.

(23) Shoyu Chicken

Chicken dips delightfully in a flavorful marinade, then, grilled to perfection for a yummy finish. The marinade is too basic and too Japanese. It is mostly about soy sauce, brown sugar, and spices. So, what are you waiting for> This makes for a great main dish, served with rice and veggie side dishes.

Yield: 12

Cooking Time: 1 hr 40 mins

List of Ingredients:

- 5 lbs. chicken thighs
- 1 cup soy sauce
- 1 cup brown sugar
- 1 pc onion, chopped
- 4 garlic cloves, minced
- 1 tablespoon fresh ginger, grated
- 1 teaspoon ground paprika
- 1 tablespoon dried oregano
- 1 teaspoon red pepper flakes, crushed
- 1 teaspoon ground cayenne pepper
- 1 tablespoon ground black pepper
- 1 cup water

MMMMMMMMMMMMMMMMMMMMMMMMMMMMMMMMMM

Methods:

1. Combine all the ingredients together in a bowl, mixing well until sugar is completely dissolved.

2. Transfer to a Ziploc bag.

3. Add chicken thighs and seal.

4. Allow to marinade inside the fridge for at least an hour or more.

5. When chicken is almost ready, preheat an outdoor grill. Grease with some cooking spray.

6. Lift chicken from the marinade and grill until cooked through, about 15 minutes each side.

7. Serve with a side of your choice.

(24) Cod Patties

Fish patties are served delightfully good in Japan. In this recipe, cod fillets, green onions, and carrots are made into a paste before it is deep-fried. It could be eaten with plain rice or as is. Just create a suitable sauce to complement the fish.

Yield: 8

Cooking Time: 30 mins

List of Ingredients:

- ¾ lb. cod fillet, diced
- 1 pc green onion, finely chopped
- 1 pc carrot, finely chopped
- 1 pc egg, lightly beaten
- ½ tablespoons sugar
- 1 tablespoon katakuriko
- 1 cup vegetable oil
- Pinch of salt

MMMMMMMMMMMMMMMMMMMMMMMMMMMMMMMMMMM

Methods:

1. Place cod fillets in the food processor, pulse until smooth.

2. Transfer fish in a bowl. Add the rest of the ingredients and mix until combined.

3. Divide fish paste into 8 portions. Form into patties and fry in hot oil over medium fire.

4. Dry in paper towels.

5. Serve as a snack or with a side dish of your choice.

(25) Japanese Braised Pork

Pork and soy sauce complement each other well and the Japanese cooks know that very well. This braised pork is a testament to how they love these two ingredients. It's a classic dish that has been around for many years, usually served during party feasts and important occasions. Pork belly is used for this recipe. Its neatly layered fat and meat presents a nice, melt-in-your-mouth texture.

Yield: 8

Cooking Time: 55 mins

List of Ingredients:

- 2 lbs. pork belly strips
- ½ cup soy sauce
- ½ cup sugar
- 1 pc onion, chopped
- 1 tablespoon vegetable oil
- ½ cup sake
- 4 pcs hardboiled eggs, peeled
- 3 pcs green onions, cut into thirds
- Japanese yellow mustard to serve

MMMMMMMMMMMMMMMMMMMMMMMMMMMMMMMMM

Methods:

1. Place pork belly strips and onion in a pressure cooker, submerged in water.

2. Bring pork to a boil over high, then, put the lid on until it builds up heat.

3. Once the pressure is on, you may reduce heat to low and cook for 30 minutes.

4. Cut up pork belly strips into 2-3 inches pieces. Discard onions and sauce.

5. Heat oil in a wok. Sauté green onions. Remove and discard when browned.

6. Add pork and brown sides before adding eggs, sake, soy sauce, and sugar.

7. Cook in a simmer for 15 minutes.

8. Serve with Japanese yellow mustard.

(26) Chilled Pork Salad

Hot summer days in Japan requires a refreshing dish. This chilled pork salad is a great option when you want something delicious that will help you endure the humidity levels. It is a favorite snack in Japan not only during summer but all seasons. The pork belly slices paired with Daikon radish and Ponzu sauce is irresistibly good.

Yield: 2

Cooking Time: 15 mins

List of Ingredients:

- ½ lb. pork belly, thinly sliced
- 1 cup Daikon radish, grated
- 2 cups mixed salad greens
- ½ cup plum tomatoes, quartered
- ½ cup Ponzu-citrus soy sauce
- 1 cup water

MMMMMMMMMMMMMMMMMMMMMMMMMMMMMMMMMM

Methods:

1. Boil water in a saucepan, add pork, and simmer for 2-5 minutes until meat changes in color.

2. Transfer meat in a bowl and set aside chilled.

3. Mix veggies in a salad bowl. Add chilled pork.

4. Toss in Ponzu-citrus sauce to coat and serve.

(27) Cabbage Rolls

Ground meat rolled in cabbage and served with seasoned soup is one of the most popular traditional Japanese recipes for its simplicity yet extravagant taste.

Yield: 4

Cooking Time: 40 mins

List of Ingredients:

- 10 leaves medium-sized cabbage
- ½ lb. ground beef
- ½ lb. ground pork
- ½ onion, chopped
- 1 pc egg, lightly beaten
- ½ cup Japanese bread crumbs
- 2 cup chicken broth
- 1 tablespoon ketchup
- 1 tablespoon tomato paste
- 1 tablespoon parsley, chopped
- Salt and pepper to taste

MMMMMMMMMMMMMMMMMMMMMMMMMMMMMMMMMM

Methods:

1. Place cabbage leaves in a microwave oven until wilted.

2. Mix together ground meats, onions, egg, and breadcrumbs. Season with salt and pepper.

3. Divide mixture into 10 portions and wrap in cabbage rolls.

4. Arrange cabbage rolls in a pot, add the rest of the ingredients, reserving parsley for garnishing.

5. Simmer for 20 minutes until sauce thickens.

6. Top with chopped parsley and serve.

Chapter IV - Japanese Dessert Recipes

MMMMMMMMMMMMMMMMMMMMMMMMMMMMMMMM

(28) Shibuya Toast

Mornings are a delightful time to enjoy Japan's traditional sweet favorites. Shibuya toast is a classic recipe that is very easy to make. It is also versatile because you can top it with anything, from ice cream to fruits to honey to cookies and others. You can even eat it any time of the day, any time you feel like giving yourself a treat. It's a favorite comfort food that is differentiated from regular toasts by its height.

Yield: 4

Cooking Time: 30 mins

List of Ingredients:

- 4-inch slab unsliced milk bread
- 1 pc ripe banana, peeled and sliced crosswise
- ½ cup assorted berries
- 1 tablespoon granulated sugar
- 3 tablespoons unsalted butter, melted
- 3 tablespoons honey, divided
- 2 tablespoons sweetened condensed milk
- ½ cup whipped cream
- 2 scoops vanilla ice cream

For garnish: assorted nuts and cookies

MMMMMMMMMMMMMMMMMMMMMMMMMMMMMMMM

Methods:

1. Preheat oven to 350 degrees F. Prepare a parchment paper lined baking sheet. Set aside.

2. Combine berries with sugar. Set aside to allow the sugar to be absorbed.

3. Create a box on the center of the bread block, leaving at least half an inch of border on all sides.

4. Cut removed part into cubes, spread generously with melted butter, and toast in the oven until golden and crisp, about 15 minutes.

5. Meanwhile, spread condensed milk on the insides of the bread block.

6. Mix crisp bread cubes with prepared berries and transfer onto bread box.

7. Drizzle with honey, then, decorate with your choice of nuts and cookies topping, a scoop of vanilla ice cream, and some whipped cream.

8. Serve.

(29) Simple Butter Mochi

Mochi is Japan's hottest dessert these days. There are a hundred and one ways cooks serve this sweet treat but for this recipe, we decided to go simple and easy so everyone will discover why mochi rocks.

Yield: 8

Cooking Time: 1 hr 10 mins

List of Ingredients:

- 1 lb. mochiko or sweet rice flour
- 1/3 cup butter
- 2 ¼ cups granulated sugar
- 2 teaspoons baking powder
- 4 pcs eggs, lightly beaten
- 1 teaspoon vanilla extract
- 1 13.5 oz. can coconut milk
- 1 12 oz. can evaporated milk
- ½ cup water
- Cooking spray

MMMMMMMMMMMMMMMMMMMMMMMMMMMMMMMM

Methods:

1. Preheat oven to 350 degrees F. Grease a 9x13 baking pan with some cooking spray.

2. Place butter and sugar together in a mixing bowl. Cream until smooth.

3. Add the rest of the ingredients, stirring until mixture becomes smooth.

4. Pour batter in prepared pan and bake for an hour.

5. Allow to cool before cutting butter mochi with a plastic knife.

(30) Anmitsu

Anmitsu is the Japanese's answer to fruit salad of the West. It is a delightful mix of fruits together with sweet beans and agar agar jelly. This is a hit among households and Japanese street food markets, especially during the warmer months of spring and summer.

Yield: 4

Cooking Time: 30 mins

List of Ingredients:

- ½ cup sweetened agar agar jelly, cut into cubes
- 1/3 cup sweet bean paste
- ½ cup sliced peaches
- 1 pc orange, peeled and sliced
- ½ cup grapes
- ¼ cup cherries
- ½ cup kiwi, peeled and sliced
- ½ apple, peeled and sliced
- ½ cup strawberries, halved
- ¼ cup water
- 2/3 cup sugar
- 1 tablespoon lemon juice

MMMMMMMMMMMMMMMMMMMMMMMMMMMMMMMMMM

Methods:

1. Heat water, sugar, and lemon juice in a saucepan over medium fire, stirring continuously until sugar is dissolved. Allow to cool and chill while preparing the fruit mix.

2. Combine fruits and jelly in a bowl. Divide into individual serving bowls.

3. Top with a scoop of sweet bean paste.

4. Pour in some syrup before serving.

(31) Sweet Pancake Sandwich

The Japanese has very unique ways to serve sweets. For pancakes, they like it stuffed with some treats in the middle for a delightful breakfast sandwich. Dorayaki is a traditional dish that is mostly about regular pancakes sandwiched with a variety of different fillings. Although anko or the sweet bean paste is commonly used, you can go creative with your filling. Use cream-based fillings with fruits, chestnuts, and other ingredients and nobody would stop you. This recipe is best served with a cup of warm Japanese green tea.

Yield: 2

Cooking Time: 30 mins

List of Ingredients:

- 1 cup all-purpose flour
- ½ teaspoons baking soda
- ¾ lb. sweet bean paste
- 2/3 cup sugar
- 2 pcs eggs
- 3 tablespoons water
- 1 tablespoon vegetable oil for frying

MMMMMMMMMMMMMMMMMMMMMMMMMMMMMMMM

Methods:

1. Whisk together sugar and eggs. Set aside.

2. Dissolve baking soda in 3 tablespoons of water. You may also use milk for a richer taste.

3. Add dissolved baking soda in eggs mixture.

4. Gradually sift flour onto the pancake batter and mix until combined, allowing a few lumps to appear.

5. Heat a lightly greased nonstick pan.

6. Pour ¼ cup of batter and cook until small bubbles appear. Turn once.

7. Allow pancakes to cool a little before adding a spoon of sweet bean paste on one side of a pair.

8. Serve.

About the Author

A native of Indianapolis, Indiana, Valeria Ray found her passion for cooking while she was studying English Literature at Oakland City University. She decided to try a cooking course with her friends and the experience changed her forever. She enrolled at the Art Institute of Indiana which offered extensive courses in the culinary Arts. Once Ray dipped her toe in the cooking world, she never looked back.

When Valeria graduated, she worked in French restaurants in the Indianapolis area until she became the head chef at one of the 5-star establishments in the area. Valeria's attention to taste and visual detail caught the eye of a local business person who expressed an interest in publishing her recipes. Valeria began her secondary career authoring cookbooks and e-books which she tackled with as much talent and gusto as her first career. Her passion for food leaps off the page of her books which have colourful anecdotes and stunning pictures of dishes she has prepared herself.

Valeria Ray lives in Indianapolis with her husband of 15 years, Tom, her daughter, Isobel and their loveable Golden Retriever, Goldy. Valeria enjoys cooking special dishes in her large, comfortable kitchen where the family gets involved in preparing meals. This successful, dynamic chef is an inspiration to culinary students and novice cooks everywhere.

•••••••••••••••••••••

Author's Afterthoughts

Thank you for Purchasing my book and taking the time to read it from front to back. I am always grateful when a reader chooses my work and I hope you enjoyed it!

With the vast selection available online, I am touched that you chose to be purchasing my work and take valuable time out of your life to read it. My hope is that you feel you made the right decision.

I very much would like to know what you thought of the book. Please take the time to write an honest and informative review on Amazon.com. Your experience and opinions will be of great benefit to me and those readers looking to make an informed choice.

With much thanks,

Valeria Ray

Made in United States
North Haven, CT
04 August 2022

22292824R00061